three-dimensional decoupage

HOW TO TRANSFORM ANY PRINT INTO AN "IN-DEPTH" PICTURE

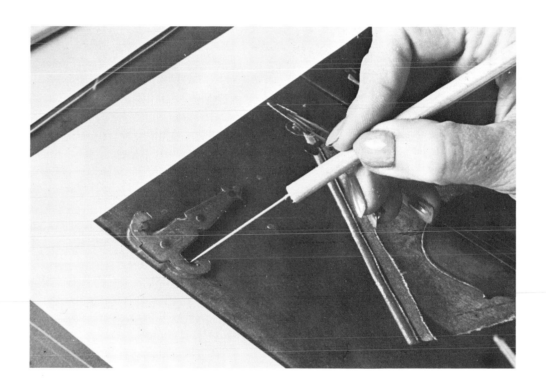

By ADELE MILLARD

PHOTOGRAPHS BY MARC FELDMAN

STERLING PUBLISHING CO., INC. NEW YORK

Oak Tree Press Co., Ltd.
London & Sydney

Contents

Dedicated
to Bud, Neal, Joan, and Holly

Acknowledgments

The author wishes to express her appreciation for the assistance so graciously given, and gratefully accepted, by Gloria Greenwald, Pearl Roen, Florence Wheeler, Bernice Hirsch, Charles Marks, and Joan Millard.

Before You Begin

THREE-DIMENSIONAL DECOUPAGE is a variation of an art that dates back to at least the 17th century. Some records indicate that Venice was the birthplace of decoupage, but experts differ over the date and place of origin.

Decoupage, a French word meaning "cutting out," originally referred to the decorating of furniture with cutouts taken from prints. Eventually anything with a surface that could be enhanced by the addition of these cutouts, including boxes, trays and accessories of any kind, was used as a background for decoupage.

Through the years there have been several resurgences of the craft. During Victorian days, japanning, as decoupage was sometimes called, became the vogue for genteel ladies who made myriads of tea trays and little boxes, profusely covered with cupids, flowers, and other symbols of that sentimental age.

It has been just within the past few years that three-dimensional decoupage in its present form has started to arouse interest in the craft and hobby fields. Originally this form of decoupage was made with a shadow box that was lined with a picture to simulate a background, and then the paper figures were moulded around wadded paper to give the illusion of dimension and placed like actors on a stage. This had a toy-like property and is quite different from the modern adaptation which uses several copies of the same picture, and by cutting, contouring, and layering achieves a depth that gives the picture its third dimension.

Many crafts call for talents that are beyond the scope of the average person. This is not true of three-dimensional decoupage, for with the proper materials, a bit of patience and a few basic rules for guidance anyone can create pictures that are both beautiful and unique. You do not need any special artistic abilities or any previous art knowledge—your ability will come with practice as you learn more about the art with each picture you make. You will find a great freedom of expression in this medium, since you are not limited to a particular period or subject—any picture that pleases you is a likely project. You can make a beautiful three-dimensional copy of Leonardo da Vinci's ''The Last Supper'' to hang above a living-room fireplace, or compose some charming Walt Disney characters into 3-D to enliven a child's bedroom. The possibilities are endless.

Almost every picture you assemble will differ from the previous one in subject, composition and detail, but the basic principles of cutting, contouring, and layering will still apply. The first picture in this book teaches you these basic procedures, and you will use them in each of the projects. As you become more proficient, your own creativity will inspire modifications and improvements to suit your concept of each picture.

Although the directions refer to the specific prints used in this book, you will find that while you may not have the same prints, you will be able to apply these directions to similar pictures very easily.

MATERIALS

All of the following materials are available at hobby shops or artists' supply houses.

a piece of heavy glass — This is what you will do your cutting on when using a knife.

hobby knife and blades

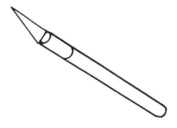

Be sure to change the blade fairly often. If it becomes dull, it will tear the print. One blade should last for the making of one complete picture. Save a couple of the old blades; they are useful for scraping dried glue off the glass.

manicure or decoupage scissors — Good for cutting round edges.

brown soft-tip pen

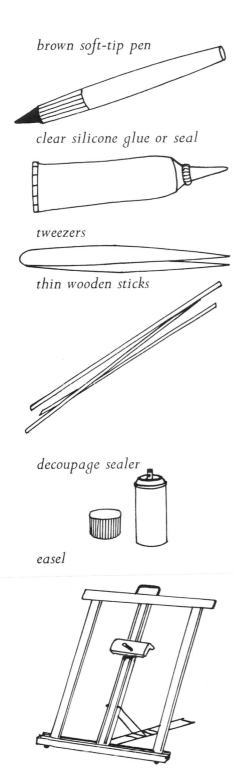

You will use this to darken all cut edges. This gives a finished look to the cut-out pieces. It is also handy for ''contouring.''

clear silicone glue or seal

You will need two sizes, large and small. This glue dries to a stiff blob, holds a cut piece away from the one underneath, and creates a mound effect.

tweezers

For cuttings that are too small for your fingers to pick up and place properly.

thin wooden sticks

These can be found in some markets in the Chinese or Japanese food section. If you cannot find them, use something like them, because they are very important in transferring the glue from the tube to the picture, removing excess glue, lifting, and for delicate aligning.

decoupage sealer

Get a large spray can as you will use it for preparing the prints for cutting and also for putting a finishing coat on the picture when you are through.

easel

A small table-top one is nice to have. Although you work with the picture down on the table, when you view it finished you see it directly in front of you, so you have to be sure that your alignment is right. If you do not have an easel, place something on the table that you can use for propping up the picture after each section is glued down. A quick glance will show you anything that has to be corrected, so that it can be done while the glue is still pliable.

Illus. 1. A simple print, such as this charming "Rag Doll by Lyn," will introduce you to almost all of the vital techniques of three-dimensional decoupage.

Illus. 2. Here is the "Rag Doll by Lyn" transformed into a new dimension!

1. "Rag Doll by Lyn"

BEGIN YOUR FIRST three-dimensional picture by buying four copies of a simple print such as the "Rag Doll by Lyn" in Illus. 1 and a heavy cardboard or Masonite sheet a little larger than the picture. For example, if the picture is 7 × 9″ (18 × 23 cm.) use an 8 × 10″ (20 × 25 cm.) backing to allow for proper matting and framing. Remember that tiny details not easily discernible in a flat picture will be brought to the viewer's attention with greater impact as a result of the added dimension. A frame that is too close to the picture hems it in and could produce an effect of clutter that would diminish the picture's importance.

Illus. 3. Begin your project by outlining one print on your cardboard or Masonite backing, which should be only slightly larger than the print, as shown here.

The depth of three-dimensional pictures necessitates shadow-box-type frames. There are ready-made ones on the market; however, you can adapt a regular frame by building up the back enough to compensate for the depth of the picture. The subject of the picture should determine the style of the frame. Modern and very detailed pictures are set off to advantage by simple framing while an 18th-century print would be enhanced by a more detailed, elaborate style.

To increase the three-dimensional effect of your framed pictures, you might also want to use a standard picture light above them.

Before you work on your prints, spray each one with decoupage sealer to prepare the paper for cutting. This not only prevents the paper from tearing but brightens the colors. *Spray each of the prints three times.* Do this lightly and evenly and lay the print on a flat surface immediately after each spraying to prevent the spray from running down the picture and leaving marks and spots. Wait about 5 minutes between sprays for the prints to dry thoroughly.

Print 1

Center one print on the backing and lightly trace its outline with a pencil as in Illus. 3. Then remove the print, and 1 inch in from the

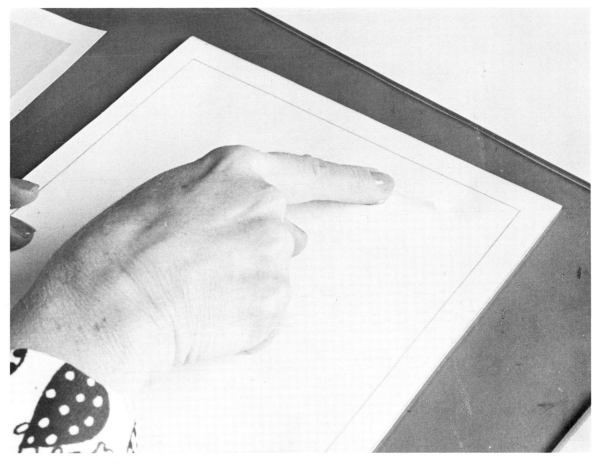

Illus. 4. Make a smooth border of silicone glue approximately 1 inch wide on the backing, following the outline of the print.

pencil outline lightly dab and smooth silicone glue up to the outline as in Illus. 4. Place the picture back in position within the outline and pat down (Illus. 5).

Now take the time to study your picture. Obviously you chose it because it appealed to you, but you must go beyond the over-all appearance and look at its composition. Look at Illus. 1 again. Determine what constitutes the background, the foreground and middle section. Is there a focal point? The background is the distant portion of the picture behind the main objects and sometimes may just be a setting for them. The fence, sunflowers, butterfly, and leaves at the base of the fence are the background in this picture. If a picture you work on has a background that is merely alluded to by

Illus. 5. Carefully place the print back on the pencilled outline, and smooth and pat so that there are no wrinkles or bumps.

faint lines and is not clearly discernible, it is best to leave it alone. However, if there are workable details, paying attention to these will be the first step towards the dimensional effect you wish to create. You should work on the background first so that you can judge what the necessary elevation for the remaining objects will be, since in most instances you want to keep the same perspective that the artist has in the picture.

The middle section is very often the focal point of the picture. Here you can readily see that the figure of the rag doll is larger and more colorful than the rest of the picture and your eye is drawn towards it.

The foreground is nearest to the eye of the viewer. Usually the

Illus. 6. The first thing you must do is determine the various elements of your picture—the foreground, the background, and the middle ground. In the "Rag Doll by Lyn," the foreground is composed of the flowers and the rabbit at the bottom of the picture.

objects are larger and the details more noticeable than those of the background. Illus. 6 shows that the foreground consists of the flowers and the rabbit. The foreground will be layered several times while the background will take just one layering so that this variance in depth will add to the perspective of the picture.

Now that you have established the elements of your picture, take a moment to become familiar with the terms used throughout this book. *Layering* in three-dimensional decoupage means glueing one copy of an object on top of another with lumps of glue. Illus. 7 shows two layers attached to the bottom print by the silicone seal, a glue that can be mounded. The amount of glue you use determines the height of the layering. You transfer the glue to the surface of the picture with one of your wooden sticks. Keep the glue away from the edges to prevent any seeping out on the surrounding area. To emphasize a detail without raising it much or in using a thin cutting that does not have enough surface to work with easily, put the glue on the cutting itself, using the smallest amount possible. It takes 5 to 10 minutes before the glue starts to dry and harden, ample time to remove any that may have seeped out under the edges or to change the alignment if necessary. The silicone seal is easy to work with and by the time you are finished with your first picture, you will be adept at using it.

Illus. 7. Here is an example of the basic technique of "layering." Layering is done with lumps of silicone glue, which you can see clearly under the two sunflowers attached to the basic print.

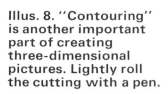

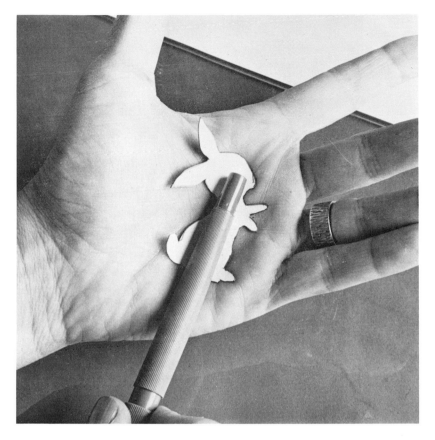

Illus. 8. "Contouring" is another important part of creating three-dimensional pictures. Lightly roll the cutting with a pen.

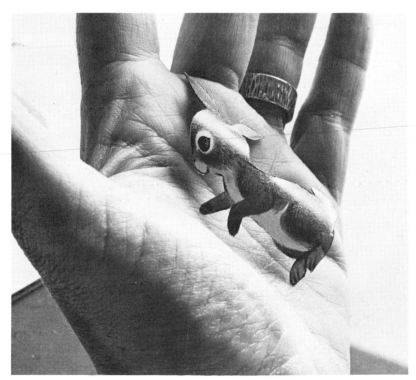

Illus. 9. Your contoured cutting should look like this. Handle it carefully so that it does not flatten out again.

Illus. 10. Every surface that you cut must be darkened with a soft-tip ink marker, so that the cut edges are not visible on the finished picture.

Illus. 8 shows what is meant by *contouring*. This is the shaping of a cutout which you do by lightly rolling the back of the object with a soft-tip pen or other similarly curved tool. Generally, you will contour figures of people and animals to give them a slightly rounded and more lifelike look. In Illus. 9 you can see how effectively this technique shapes the figure of the rabbit.

Outlining every cut surface with your soft-tip pen and darkening the edges give each cutout a finished look and help it to blend with the portion of the picture to which it is layered. Without this coloring you would readily notice all the cuts in the picture and this would detract from the over-all effect. Place the cutting face-down on the glass and go over every edge with the pen so that no white edge remains as shown in Illus. 10. (The term "cutting" is used to

Illus. 11. In order to avoid having the paper slip when doing delicate work, always do small details and thin-line cutting first.

denote the object which has been cut out.) When you have finished, pick up the cutting and holding it with the back towards you, slowly turn it round so that you can see all sides and check for white places that the pen may have missed. Always work with the back of the cutting when you are shading it—should your pen slip (and it will do so occasionally) there is no chance of marking up the front of the picture.

Do your cutting with the hobby knife on top of the glass. Always do all delicate work, such as cutting within thin lines, first. Illus. 11 shows cutting round the stalks of the sunflowers before removing anything else from the print. In this way, you work with a whole piece of paper and there is less chance of the paper slipping and causing you to cut through a line.

Print 2

Your first print is glued to the back-board and now you are ready to cut into your second print. Cut out the background including the figure of the rag doll and the watering can. This gives you one straight piece to layer. Cutting the fence around the figure would give you smaller pieces that are difficult to glue and to keep level. Next, cut the foreground of the flowers and the rabbit. Illus. 12 shows the two

Illus. 12. From your second print, cut out the elements of your picture separately. Here are the background and the foreground parts of the "Rag Doll by Lyn."

Illus. 13. This is about as much glue as you will need for a contact point. However, you will want to vary the amount at times, depending on how elevated you feel a cutting should be.

sections. Darken the edges of the two pieces and they are ready to be layered.

Illus. 13 shows the average amount of glue to use for one contact point. The contact points for placing the glue are shown in Illus. 14 and 15. You will develop your own preference for either placing the glue directly on the print or on the cutting itself. The size and shape of the area you are layering usually determines which method you use; the convenient way is the best.

The background section is ready to be glued down. Be sure that

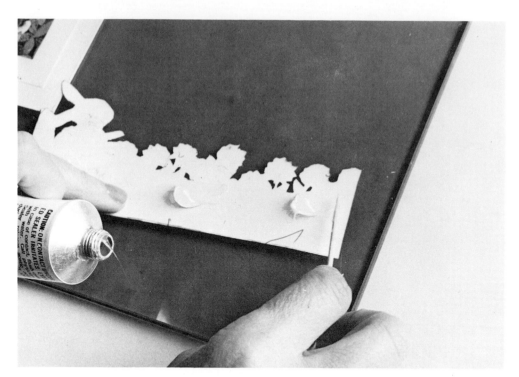

Illus. 14. Here are the appropriate contact points for the foreground of the "Rag Doll by Lyn."

Illus. 15. The background requires more contact points. For some areas, you may prefer to place the glue on the print, rather than on the cutting itself.

Illus. 16. When your background is ready to be glued, carefully align it over the basic print and lower it slowly into place.

Illus. 17. As soon as the glue makes contact with the basic print, set the picture up on your easel so that you are looking straight at it, not down on it. If it is not in perfect alignment, use a thin stick to shift the cutting into place.

Illus. 18. When the background is firmly in place, prepare the foreground, and then put it down in the same fashion as you did the background.

your picture is lying flat on the glass, and then line up the cutting with its counterpart underneath. Set it down near enough for the glue to make contact with the underside (Illus. 16). When it is in place, prop the picture up on your easel (Illus. 17) to check on the alignment. Use a thin stick or similar tool to do any moving that is necessary to make the print and top cutting appear as one.

Do not cut out the cobblestone path as part of either section because it is not to be layered. Using only the path in the basic picture helps to create a depth division between the foreground and background.

Use the same methods for layering the foreground as shown in Illus. 18.

Illus. 19. Now you are ready for your third print. Here, the figure, the sunflowers, the butterfly, and the watering can are cut from the background. Glue the sunflowers first.

Print 3

From the third print, cut out the rag doll, the sunflowers with stems that extend from the fence, the butterfly, and the watering can. Cut out the foreground section again in one piece, but this time remove the spaces between the leaves and the flowers. This gives them more emphasis and shows a defined shape. Darken the edges of the pieces and then contour the rag doll in the same way as the rabbit was done in Illus. 8.

The practical sequence of glueing is from top to bottom and from background to foreground. Glue the sunflowers first (Illus. 19) followed by the butterfly, the rag doll, and the watering can (Illus. 20). Then elevate the foreground during glueing so that it is noticeably higher than the other elements in the picture. Illus. 21 shows the depth produced by this last layering.

Illus. 20.

Illus. 21.

Illus. 22. With your fourth and last print, you can work on whatever little details strike your fancy, such as separating the petals on the sunflowers.

Print 4

The basic elements are in place and the picture is now three-dimensional. Here you are ready for the last print, and it is now that you can give full scope to your imagination and creativity. Working with the other prints makes you thoroughly familiar with all the details of the picture, so that by now you have definite thoughts on what finishing touches will add interest and charm to the picture.

Study Illus. 1 again. Notice the way the figure is dressed. Cutting

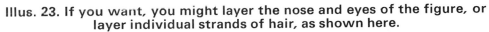

Illus. 23. If you want, you might layer the nose and eyes of the figure, or layer individual strands of hair, as shown here.

out the clothes and reassembling them on the figure produce a doll-like quality that is attractive. The sunflowers become more noticeable when you cut out the flower and separate the petals as in Illus. 22. Cut out some individual leaves at the base of the fence, contour them so they curl, and then add them to the picture. Do the same with the flowers and leaves in the foreground. Add a little extra glue to several of the flowers so that there is a difference in levels.

It is not advisable to work on facial features of simulated real people but since this is a fantasy figure you can cut out the eyes and layer them for prominence. You can also cut strands of the "yarn" hair and pull them up and away from the head as in Illus. 23. Separating the head and outer section of the rabbit and then layering it makes it a truly three-dimensional figure (Illus. 24).

All these added touches give the picture a finished, professional look. A final spray with the decoupage sealer and your first picture is ready to be matted, as in Illus. 2, and then framed.

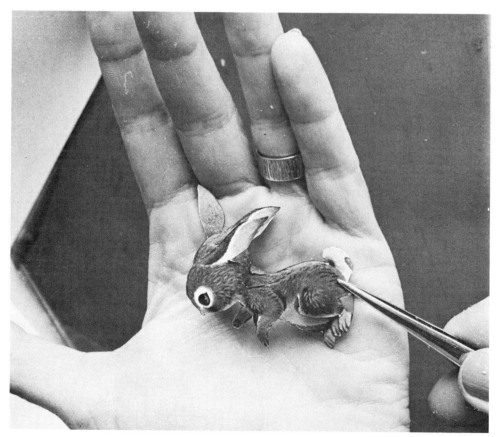

Illus. 24. The bunny gets a final layering of his various pieces to put the finishing three-dimensional touch on the picture.

2. Flowers

Pictures of flowers are among the most beautiful for three-dimensional decoupage. They are easy to work with and the finished picture rivals nature's product in realism. Some compositions of flowers are even more attractive when set on a material background. Compare the roses in Illus. 25 and Illus. 26. Silks or other slick material would be difficult to work on; however, velvet, felt, and various cotton cloths are fine and there are many colors and patterns to choose from to complement your print.

The transferring of the rose to the black velvet is a simple process. Use four copies of your print. It is not necessary to mat a material-backed picture, so make a back-board larger than you would ordinarily use. The rose print picture is 8 × 10" (20 × 25 cm.) and the backing is 10 × 12" (25 × 30 cm.). Cut a piece of black velvet to size and glue it down.

Print 1

Cut out the entire rose from the print and center it on the velvet. The use of several straight pins to outline the cutting is helpful, so that when the flower is removed and the glue is placed on the back, the pins offer some guidance in returning it to the proper place on the material (Illus. 27). You must use care in glueing since most materials will spot if any glue is dropped on them. To avoid this and because one's hands are never quite clean enough to come in constant contact with some materials, make a frame round the picture with strips of clear plastic (Illus. 28). Use four strips and bring them as close as you can to the cutout. Tack them down with pins. Plastic is the most satisfactory material for such a frame because it is thin enough not to interfere with close or delicate work.

Copyright Rose Products Co., Reno, Nevada. Painting by Anne Hershenburgh.

Illus. 25. You will find prints of flowers are among the most exciting subjects to project into the third dimension.

Illus. 26. The rose in Illus. 25 has not only had a new dimension added, but a new background of black velvet. Transferring prints to a different background often enhances their beauty, as you can see here.

Illus. 27. When transferring to a fabric or other material background, cut out the entire picture and make an outline of it on the new backing with pins. The pins serve as guidelines.

Illus. 28. To keep the material clean and free from spots of glue while you are working, make a frame of clear plastic round the print like this.

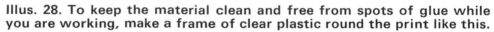

Illus. 29. Now is the time to cut out tiny details from your second print which you will use for the last layering. After you do so, set them aside, and place the glue on the first print.

Print 2

Cut out the complete rose from this print. Notice that there are little drops of water printed on several of the petals and one leaf. These are a nice touch for the finished picture. Any extra details such as these that can be used on the last layer of the picture are usually removed from the second print and set aside for when they are needed. This is the time to do it because more layers will be added and the missing portions will be covered and not noticed. Remove the water drops, put aside, and place the glue on the *first* rose as in Illus. 29. Set the second rose on the first and align the flower as in Illus. 30.

Print 3

Cut out the rose head separately from the third print. Place it upside down in the palm of your hand and contour just enough to give it a slightly rounded and raised look. Layer. Remove the leaves in clusters from the main stem. Crease each leaf just enough to take away the flat look and attach to the stem on the main picture as in Illus. 31.

Illus. 31.

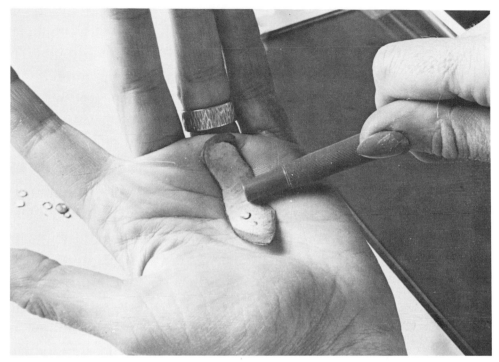

Illus. 32. Spray your last print before cutting so that you will not stain the material background. Now contour each flower petal before glueing.

Illus. 33. After glueing, you can add more contours by using a tweezers to bend the edges of the petals up or down.

Print 4

Spray the last print *before* cutting, since you cannot spray the print when it is on the material as it may leave spots. Then cut all the petals from the rose following the artist's lines. Contour each petal before glueing it into place (Illus. 32). However, reverse every other petal and contour face-up. This process makes the petals curl in opposite directions and you get a more natural look. If you cannot get the exact effect you need by contouring alone, place the petals, let the glue harden, and then take tweezers and lightly bend the edges of the petals as in Illus. 33 and 34.

Next, cut out each leaf, contour, and glue. Now add the water drops from Print 2 and your picture is finished (Illus. 26).

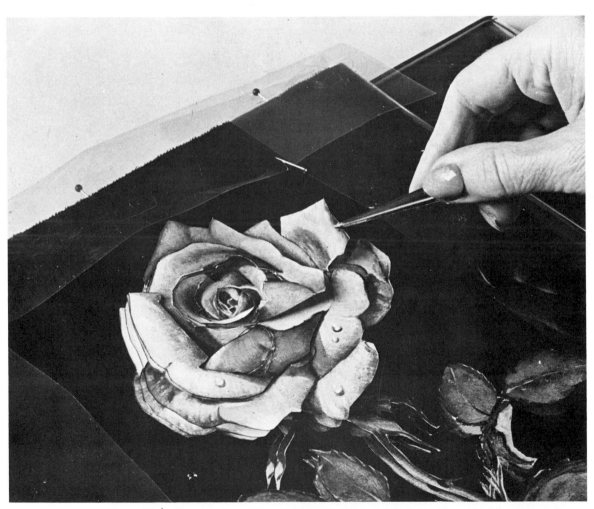

Illus. 34. Glue each petal and leaf in place. If you cut out the water drops from Print 2, this is the time to add them, as well as any other little details you saved from that print.

DAISIES

Another example of transferring flowers to material is shown in Illus. 35 and 36. Illus. 36 shows also how, by rearranging both the composition and the subject matter, you can create a new design. It is fun to be creative and you will find that sometimes a picture you like very much is not quite right for the area in which you plan to use it. A little imagination, a few minor changes, and you will have exactly what you are looking for. Here you will need four copies of the print.

Print 1

Illus. 35 shows four daisies in a line. The size of the picture is 8 × 17″ (20 × 43 cm.). The velvet-covered back-board has been enlarged to 11 × 18″ (28 × 46 cm.). Cut the entire cluster of flowers from the first print. Remove the top daisy and tuck its stem into the last leaf on the bottom of the picture. Glue the daisies to the velvet.

Print 2

Cut whole flowers and leaves from the second print. Remove the orange ''eyes'' and put them aside. Lightly roll the tips of the petals over your pen in the direction of their shape for the start of contouring at this level. Glue down.

Print 3

When cutting the flowers from the third print, cut each of the petals in to the middle, and then contour each petal. Cut away the leaves from the stems, and crease before glueing. When you glue the daisy heads, twist them around until they are in positions different from the bottom layer in order to make the flowers appear to be double blossoms.

Print 4

Use the fourth print to choose individual petals for each daisy. Place them in a random manner, making sure the ends are close to the orange ''eyes.'' When you contour the ''eyes'' that you cut out of Print 2, contour them face-down so that they appear raised, and then layer them. After the glue dries, fluff the petals out to the desired height.

Illus. 35. These daisies are about to get a face-lifting! See Illus. 36 for the results.

"Ebony and White Floral." Courtesy Arthur A. Kaplan Co., Inc., New York City.

Illus. 36. See page 33 to find out how this impressive new arrangement was accomplished.

Courtesy Bernard Picture Co., Inc., New York.

ORIENTAL MAGNOLIAS

PAINTED BY COUNTESS ZICHY

Illus. 37. You will need four prints to turn this bowl of magnolias into the stunning three-dimensional picture in Illus. 38.

Illus. 38. Here, the bowl of magnolias has been transferred to a cream-colored, textured matboard and framed in soft green which picks up the color of the leaves.

ORIENTAL MAGNOLIAS

Four prints are needed for the bowl of magnolias in Illus. 37, which shows the original print with a dark background. It is a lovely picture; however, to achieve a more effective contrast the arrangement has been transferred and re-assembled on a cream-colored, textured matboard (Illus. 38).

Cut out the first print and center it on the board. Angle your pins and they will be as effective in outlining the arrangement on the stiff board as they are on material.

To re-create the basic concept of the picture you must cut through the branches and blossoms in order to obtain whole units for the last layering. Do this by working with the three remaining prints at the same time. Cut as many whole units as you can from each print. You can glue the flowers, buds, and branches that have been cut through or have had pieces removed from them during the first and second layerings to give the depth and elevations needed. All the imperfections will be covered up by the last layering. When the glue is dry, spray the picture several times with your decoupage sealer to give the picture a high gloss.

PANSIES

The subtle background of the picture of the pansies in Illus. 39 is exactly right for the colors of the flowers, so use the basic print instead of transferring to another background. Use four prints in all, and do the first two layerings simply by cutting out the flowers and leaves and glueing in place. To be sure that proper accent is on the flowers, layer the leaves just two times. Make your creases and contours on the second layering.

Pansy faces have distinct markings and lines that divide the parts of the petals. Cut along these lines in the fourth print and shape them freely before assembling them in place. Adjust the amount of glue you use so that there is a variance in the elevation of the flowers. A lavender mat complements the colors in the picture and does much to enhance the over-all effect.

Illus. 39. The soft background of the original print was used here instead
of a substitute backing.

Illus. 40. Now, try out your newly acquired three-dimensional skills on a print combining flowers and birds, such as this one showing two blue-birds perched on a dogwood branch. (See Illus. 42 for the finished picture.)

3. Bluebirds and Dogwood

PICTURES OF BIRDS fit into any kind of décor and consequently are among the most popular prints used for three-dimensional work. Often the birds are combined with blossoms, a bright addition that adds greatly to the charm of the picture. Illus. 40 shows how the flowers give balance to the figures of the birds and how the white blossoms and green leaves heighten the birds' colors. You will need five prints.

Print 1

Glue the first print to the back-board.

Print 2

Remove the spaces between the leaves, flowers, and birds and then cut out the entire picture in one piece from the second print and layer (Illus. 41). This is the only layering for the tree branch, so be

Illus. 41.

Illus. 42.

Illus. 43. When handling thin branches which will not accommodate large mounds of glue, place your mounds as close as possible on an adjoining area, such as on the flowers and the birds here.

sure that you raise it sufficiently. Since the branch is thin and cannot carry enough glue to elevate properly, mound a larger amount of glue on the flowers and parts of the birds close to the branch (Illus. 43) and a smaller mound on the remaining portions. Subsequent layerings will build the other sections to a height that will balance the height of the branch.

Print 3

Cut out the birds and each of the flowers individually along with any leaves or stems that are attached to them. Lightly shape each flower with your tool and give a slight contour to both birds by placing them face-down in your hand and rolling the pen over the widest section of each bird. Glue the birds a little higher than the

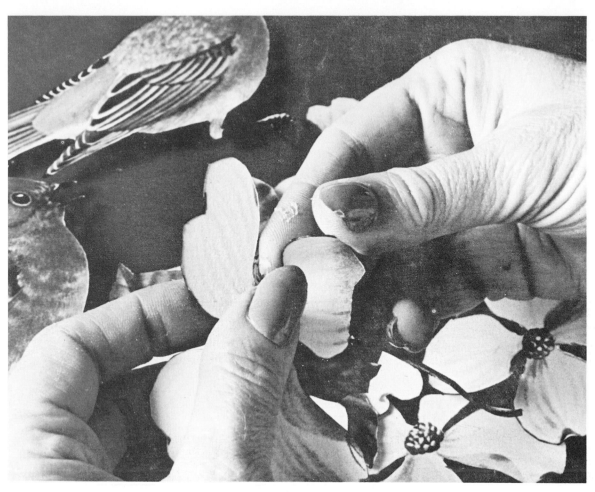

Illus. 44. From your fourth print, cut out each one of the flowers separately and also cut each petal right down to the "eye." Contour each one with either a tool or your fingers so that they do not all look exactly alike.

flowers as you layer, but be sure the claws are resting on the branches.

Print 4

Remove all the leaves. Cut out each of the flowers, cutting the petals down to the middle. Shape both the leaves and the flowers. Do some with a tool and some with your fingers to achieve a variety of forms (Illus. 44). Cut along the lines that represent the separations between the tail feathers before removing the birds from the print. Cut out and contour the birds, and after they are glued in place, check to see that the tail feathers are not bunched together and the separations are easily noticed.

Print 5

Cut out the wings of the birds in sections according to their levels. The very top section will have the head and beak attached as shown in Illus. 45. Contour each level of the wings so that they build up to the head portion (Illus. 46).

Remove the middle section of each flower and random petals of the flowers. Shape and glue.

Illus. 46.

Robe à retroussis

Illus. 47. As fashionable as this lady is, she will be even more stylish when brought up-to-date with a three-dimensional look.

GERDA·WEGENER·

Robe à retroussis

Illus. 48. And here she is—with a brand-new background, too. Notice how
the soft blue enhances the entire picture. (See page 48.)

4. 1914 Paris Model

THE CHIC YOUNG WOMAN in Illus. 47 is modelling a Parisian costume that was stylish in 1914. Illus. 47 shows the beige background used in the fashion magazine where the drawing originally appeared. With this print you will use a background substitution to give added interest. The entire composition of the picture will be enhanced by changing the beige to a soft blue as you can see in Illus. 48. You will need four prints for this project.

Print 1

Make a blue back-board the exact size of the picture. Then cut out the background, but leave the frame-work of the print, as well as the base and the figure and shrubs attached to the base. Illus. 49 shows part of the reverse side of the cutout and the amount of glue needed to make it adhere to the backing.

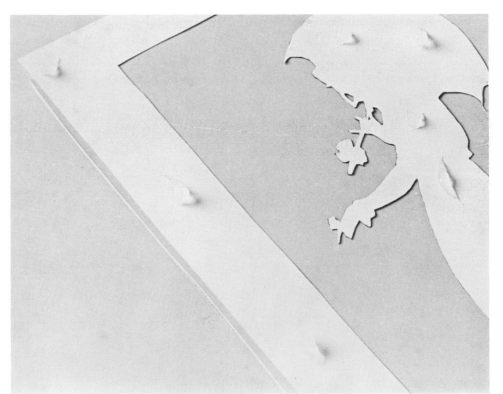

Illus. 49.

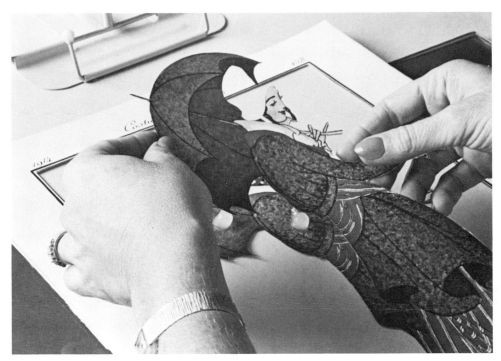

Illus. 50. Here, details such as the hat and the bow on the umbrella have
been removed from Print 2.

Illus. 51. The entire figure, the base and the shrubs from Print 2 are being
put into place.

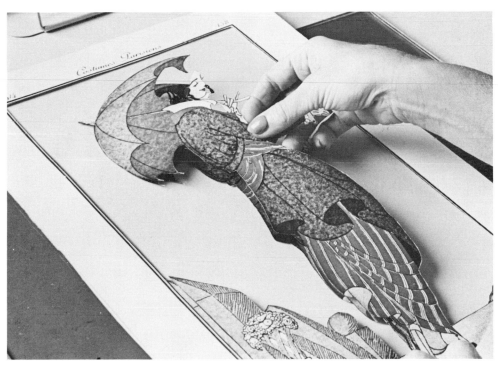

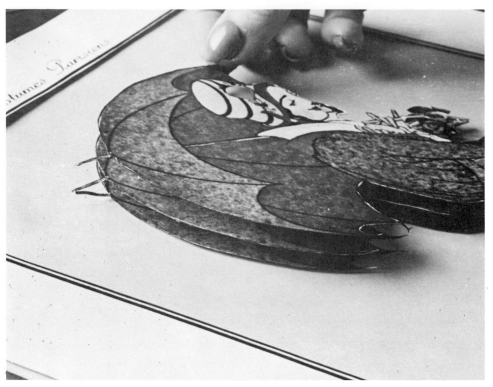

Illus. 52. From Print 3, the figure is removed from the base and layered. The rest of the pieces are cut separately and set aside for finishing touches.

Print 2

From this print, cut out the hat, the butterfly on the lady's finger and the bow on the umbrella stick (Illus. 50). These detail pieces will be used for the last print and can be put aside for the time being. Now remove the figure, base and shrubs from the print in one piece and glue at an elevated level (Illus. 51).

Print 3

Cut out the shrubs individually, as well as the flowers in the jardinière. Remove the rose from the hat and also the rose from the bow on the umbrella handle, and set aside. Now cut the figure away from the base and layer as in Illus. 52.

Print 4

Cut out the entire dress in separate sections according to the lines and folds of the costume. Remove the face, hands, shoes and outer

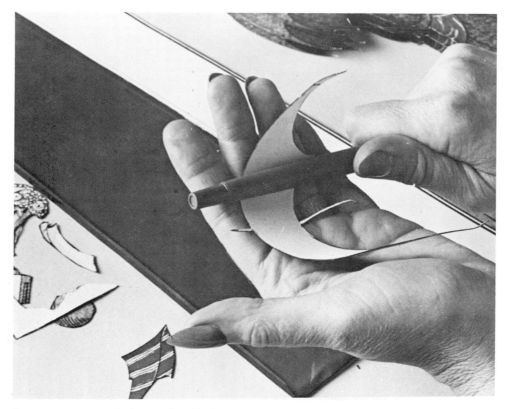

Illus. 53. Here the outer part of the umbrella is contoured. This cutting is from Print 4. Notice all of the small cuttings which are removed from this print. Be sure to remove shoes, the face, and the hands from this print.

portion of the umbrella. Shape the umbrella so that it curves out from the middle (Illus. 53). Cut out the shadowed areas of the shrubs. Remove the spaces between the lattice-work in the jardinière before lifting that section from the print.

Begin to re-assemble the costume on the figure by first contouring each of the pieces (Illus. 54). Start at the bottom of the skirt and add the sections according to the way the folds lie. Vary the amount of glue you use. The folds on the bottom of the skirt need a small amount while the over-skirt needs larger mounds for more elevation (Illus. 55). Using your tweezers, continue to add the overlying units.

Add the face (Illus. 56), and when the glue dries, add the hat from Print 2 which you have contoured (Illus. 57) so that it is slightly raised above the face. Next, glue in place the shrub sections and jardinière as shown in Illus. 58. This will give the bottom dress folds time to harden so that you can add the shoes without fear of moving

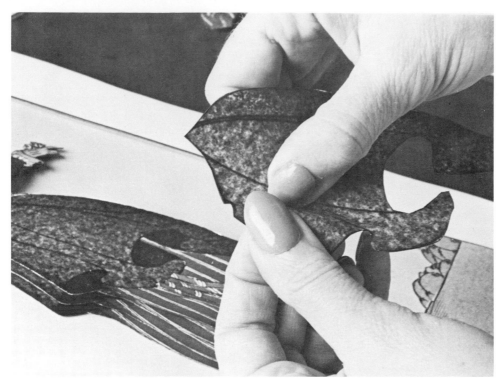

Illus. 54. Before re-assembling the pieces, contour each one.

Illus. 55. Be sure to vary the amount of glue you use in order to achieve effective differences in height, such as here where the billowing overskirt requires greater mounds.

Illus. 56. Add the face, and then the hat . . .

Illus. 57. . . . which you must first contour.

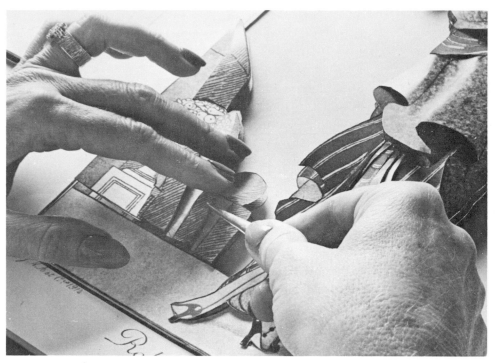

Illus. 58. After adding the face and the hat, glue in place the shrub sections and jardinière.

Illus. 59. By this time, the skirt parts will have had time to dry thoroughly, so you can add the shoes without fear of jarring anything out of place.

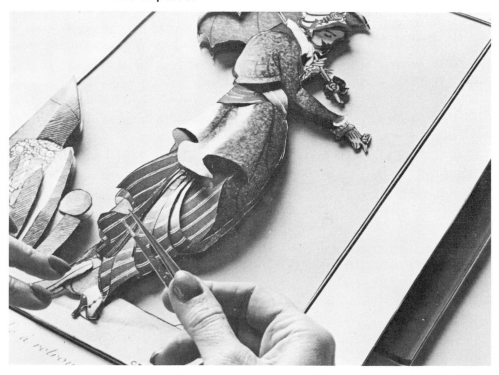

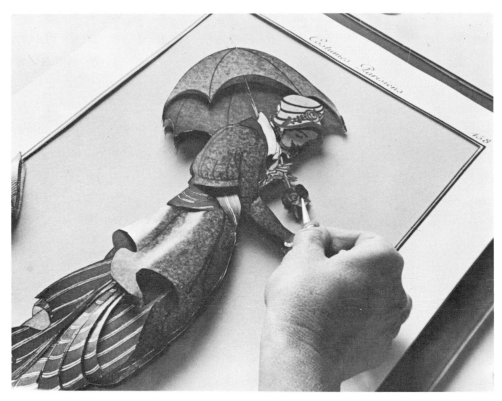

Illus. 60. Now add your final detail pieces from Prints 2 and 3. Be sure to contour the roses on both the hat and the umbrella before glueing.

anything out of place (Illus. 59). Add the other detail pieces from Print 2—the butterfly and the bow on the umbrella handle. Then curve the roses from Print 3 and add to the hat and bow on the umbrella as the final touch (Illus. 60). Spray with sealer, and your three-dimensional picture is complete.

Pictures of people are enhanced by the treatment you give to the clothes they are wearing. When working with people, be sure to study the first print carefully. Decide how many layers you want for certain articles of clothing. Then check to be sure you have enough prints. Use your second print for the extras you desire and set them aside for the last layering. Remember to shape certain parts of clothing so that they conform naturally to a figure, as you did in this picture.

5. Still-Life Paintings

PRINTS OF STILL-LIFE paintings present an interesting study in balanced design and the harmonious relationship between the subjects the artist has chosen. They lend themselves well to three-dimensional decoupage. You will be working with fine designs in shape, color, and texture. The guidelines for your cuttings and elevations are already there, and you merely have to follow them. However, with these paintings, you still have an opportunity to put in your own innovations which you can do without disturbing the balance of the original composition.

"THE OLD CREMONA"

Illus. 63 shows an arrangement of a violin, music book, and bow. You will use four prints for this project.

Illus. 61. Remove the parts in these units from Print 2.

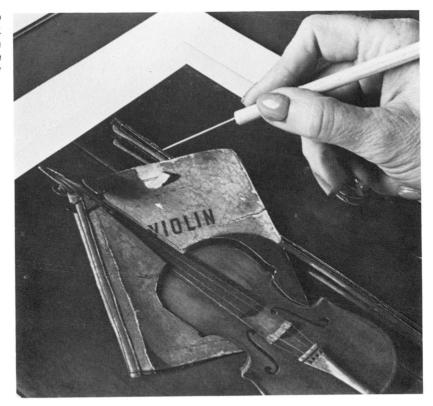

Illus. 62. Glue on the two sections of the book from Print 2. When adding the violin, be sure to elevate it slightly above the book.

Print 2

After glueing your first print to the backing, cut all the units out of the second print. By cutting out the violin, you will cut the book into two sections. Leave the bow attached to the music book. Illus. 61 shows how the units are removed. Layer the background items— hinges, lock and knob—just this once (Illus. 61). Glue the two sections of the music book (Illus. 62) and then elevate the violin slightly above the book when you set it in place.

Print 3

Cut out the violin and the music book. Discard the bow as you will cut it in two pieces which would spoil the effect you are going to achieve for the last layering. Cut out the scrollwork on the violin, (Illus. 65) following the design so that it looks like Illus. 66. Run your knife point down the left side of the music book to simulate the tear line and then cut out the tear and the tatters on the rest of the book. Set them aside as you will layer the elements from both the third and fourth prints at the same time.

WILLIAM M. HARNETT — THE OLD CREMONA

Courtesy Bernard Picture Co., Inc., New York.

Illus. 63. Here is the original print. The title, ''The Old Cremona,'' refers to the make of violin, in the same way as does the more familiar ''Stradivarius,'' both of which were made by Antonio Stradivarius of Cremona, Italy.

58

Illus. 64. Prints of still-life paintings are a challenge to your imagination. You might find that you can think of innovative details that the artist overlooked!

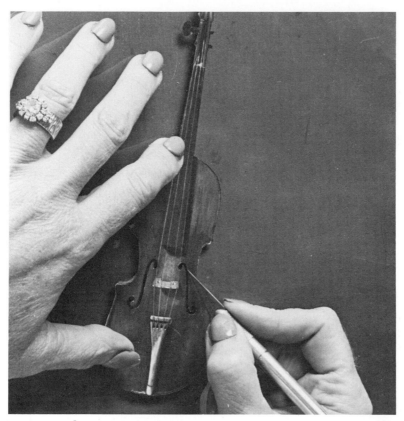

Illus. 65. Carefully cut out the scrollwork on the violin so that it . . .

Illus. 66. . . . looks like this.

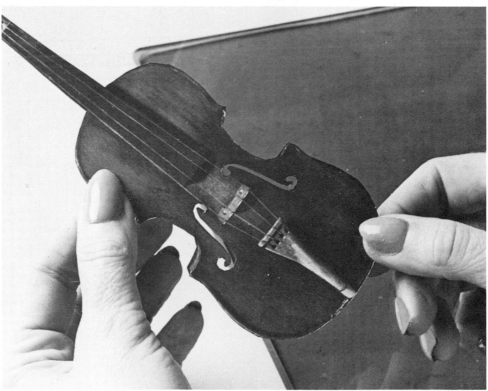

Print 4

From this print cut out the component parts of the violin: the tailpiece, the bridge, and the curved scroll above the pegbox at the top. Cut out the bow, going right through the music book so that the bow is one piece. Now take a thick needle such as one that is used for crewelwork and run it through each of the holes in the tailpiece.

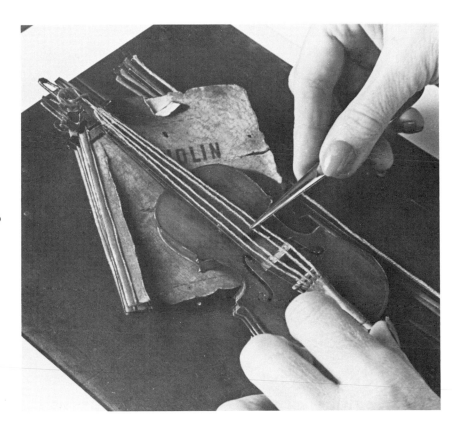

Illus. 67. Use brown embroidery thread to make the violin strings.

To make the violin strings, take four strands of brown embroidery thread, start each one from the back of the tailpiece, knot them so that they cannot slip through, and push each through a hole to the front. Now glue the tailpiece and bridge to the violin and set it aside for the glue to dry.

Take three more strands of thread, double them so you have a workable thickness, and glue to the bow. Use tiny dabs of glue on the existing bow line to hold the strands in place nicely. Glue the bow to the music book that is layered on the picture. Now you can glue the music book from the third print, using large dabs of glue to give

Illus. 68.

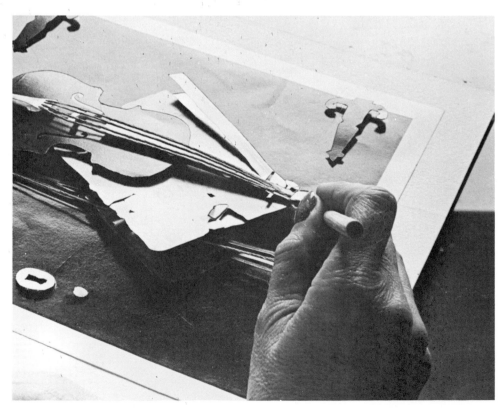

Illus. 69.

it height. Layer the violin and also raise it by using larger amounts of glue.

Pull the strands of thread tautly up to the top of the violin and then glue them down (Illus. 67). Illus. 68 and 69 show how to place the curved scroll piece over the ends of the thread, and the tatters and the tear from Print 3.

Spray with sealer (Illus. 70) and mat with a pale green matting that matches the color of the music book and the picture is complete and ready to be framed.

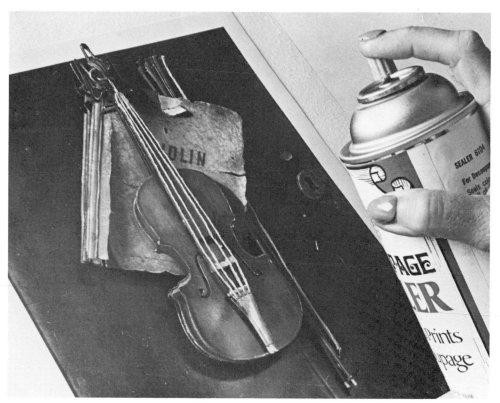

Illus. 70. Before matting your finished picture, spray with decoupage sealer.

TEA KETTLE

Simple objects can make a pleasing arrangement as shown in Illus. 71 of a tea kettle with fruit and nuts, an ideal picture for a kitchen. This is not a complicated picture and can be composed in a few hours.

Use three prints. Glue your basic print to the back-board, and then cut the wallboards of the background out of the second print, removing the cracks between the boards, and glue into place. Cut out all the units and then layer the table so that it rests against the back and is raised in front. Remove the cover, handle, and spout from the kettle and set aside. Leave the fruits and nuts in clusters. Then glue the kettle and dish into place.

Cut out the kettle intact from the third print. Remove the fruit in one piece and then separate them and contour. Layer the kettle and dish. Then add the cover, handle and spout. Glue the fruit clusters from Print 2 close to their counterparts. When the glue holding the clustered fruit is set, add the individual fruit. Cut out the edge of the table, bend it at the left corner, and then glue down.

Illus. 71 (opposite page). Here is a still life that should arouse your creative instincts. Can you imagine what this old-fashioned tea kettle print will look like in the third dimension?

6. Collectibles on an Étagère

You WILL NEED five prints for the picture in Illus. 72. Glue Print 1 down on your back-board.

Print 2

You can give this nostalgic collection a dramatic touch by a simple device after cutting out the second print, as shown in Illus. 73 and 74. Use a ruler to bend the left and right side edges of the shelves towards you. After you position this on the basic print, you will see how effectively it adds to the depth of the picture.

Print 3

Cut out the top and bottom shelves. Leave all the items on the

Illus. 72. There's a wealth of detail in this print, so you will need five copies.

Illus. 73. Here is a special technique for adding greater depth to a picture of this kind. Lay a ruler along the side edges of the shelves.

Illus. 74. Then, bend the edges up towards you like this.

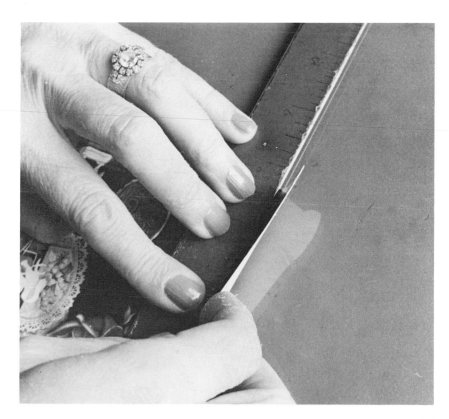

Illus. 75. The finished picture. Notice the depth of the sides of the shelves.

shelves and remove the spaces between each article. When glueing, slant the shelves towards the back of the picture and manipulate the side edges of Print 2 so that they fit snugly against the shelves.

Print 4

Remove all the keepsakes from this print, and layer.

Print 5

From the fifth print, cut each of the rose petals, contour and glue in position on the flower. Contour or crease the leaves and add. Cut the valentine apart and re-assemble the sections at different elevations. Remove the inner portion of the double frame and replace with clear plastic. Separate the fan into two sections and crease the top part along the existing lines. Re-assemble when layering.

7. Parlour Musicians

THE DELIGHTFUL LADIES intent on their musical performance in Illus. 76, will show up well in three dimensions. This picture is easier to compose than the finished picture might lead you to believe (Illus. 80).

You will need four prints. Glue the first to a back-board. The beginning emphasis in assembling this picture is in your treatment of the walls of the room.

Print 2

Start by cutting out the figures of the woman and the girl complete with the articles they are attached to from the second print

Courtesy Arthur A. Kaplan Co., Inc., New York City.

Illus. 76. You will need four prints to make this picture three-dimensional. (See page 72.)

Illus. 77. From your second print, cut out the two figures, along with every object to which they are actually attached. Study it carefully first so you do not miss any parts.

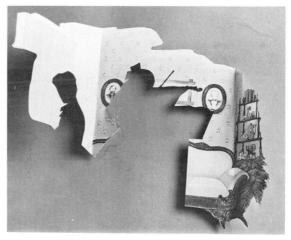

Illus. 78. Then, from the same print, cut out what is left of the walls. Crease the two corners of the walls, using a ruler as you did on page 67.

(Illus. 77). Set them aside as you will use them in reverse order with the cuttings from Print 3.

Continue cutting the second print by removing what is left of the walls as shown in Illus. 78. Notice also in this illustration that the two corners of the walls have been creased. The back is flat and both sides angle towards the front. Glue this section to the base print. Make sure that your side walls are not over-emphasized. A slight angle is enough without disturbing the balance of the picture.

Print 3

Cut out the figures and all the objects in one piece (Illus. 79). Use enough glue to give a raised effect and layer. Then glue the units taken from Print 2 and layer them.

Print 4

Use this print for the details that will enhance the three-dimensional character of the picture. Cut out the pictures on the back and left side of the wall and layer. Cut the drape from the curtain rod, crease along the fold lines, and hang in place. Cut the outer edge of the door moulding and raise just a fraction when glueing.

Cut out the entire sleeve and arm of the lady playing the piano, contour to give fullness to the puffed sleeve, and when glued in place, raise her hand over the keyboard. Cut and add the sheet music, creased down the middle, to the piano. Remove the objects on the round table and place an indentation in the middle of the yellow roses before layering.

Cut out the young girl's arm holding the violin bow and attach separately. Cut and add the collar to her dress, and cut the bottom

Illus. 79. Cut, in one piece, the figures and objects from Print 3.

Illus. 80. Here is the finished picture, right down to the last detail—even the ferns have been cut so that they feather out!

half of her dress along the top of the pink sash. Fold in some creases and layer. Cut out the sofa seat, the doily, and all the wood trim, and layer on the sofa.

Cut out the dog and then cut round his ear so that you can raise it with a mound of glue. Glue the dog down. The curio shelves, along with the ferns that have been feathered by cutting between the fronds, add the final touch.

As you can see, this picture allows for as much creativity as you choose to give it. And, as in most of your three-dimensional work, the more you do, the greater the feeling of realism.

8. A White House

THIS CHARMING SCENE will show you several techniques that are new to you. Once you have learned them, you will find yourself using them over and over again in working on other pictures because of the realistic effects you can achieve. It will take five prints to complete the picture.

Illus. 81.

Courtesy Arthur A. Kaplan Co., Inc., New York City.

Study Illus. 81 and note the divisions of background, middle area, and foreground. The lighter part of the picture behind the house and large tree is the background. The house and tree are the focal points, and the lawn, path, fence and shrubbery are the foreground. However, in this picture, before you start any divisional cutting, you will work on the windows first. This calls for delicate cutting so the picture must be intact to avoid slippage (you will be applying the same principle here as in cutting the sunflowers in the ''Rag Doll by Lyn''on page 15).

The windows are cut differently in each of three prints so that in the final picture you will be able to look into the windows just the way you would in a real house.

Glue your first print to the back-board.

Print 2

As shown in Illus. 82, begin on this print with the windows. Cut away the empty spaces and any objects that you can see inside. Do not cut out the curtains or the shades. The frames dividing the panes of glass are very thin, so cut carefully—do not try to go to the exact line but stop your cutting a fraction before reaching it. You will find it easier if you move your print round slowly as you cut. This technique takes some of the pressure off the hand holding the knife so there is less chance of cutting through the lines. Do all the windows except the one in the dormer on top of the roof and the window in the door.

Illus. 83 shows how to cut out the second print from the back-

Illus. 82.

Illus. 83.

ground. Begin at the bush on the upper left of the picture and cut the dark portion of the grass in an uneven, up-and-down motion. Do both sides of the house, cutting round the bushes and being sure to get the tiny section behind the porch. The uneven cutting simulates the appearance of grass when seen from a distance and emphasizes the elevation of this section of the picture.

Remove the dormer window next. You will need it for your last print, so set it aside. Next, cut out the house and the tree and swing, leaving the points of contact with the grass uncut. As you can see in Illus. 83, the outline of the tree is irregular.

Cut out the path. Cut through the connecting sections so that this part of the picture is free from the print. Turn the picture over and lightly roll the grass with your pen or knife from the middle to the edges. Then, with your fingers, turn the edges down just a little. When you glue this section to the base print, the grass verges on the path with just a tiny lift between them, and will appear to be growing right up to the pathway.

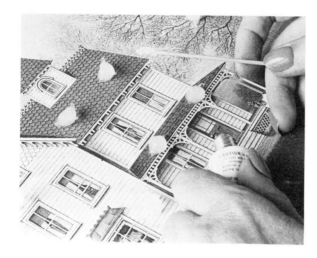

Illus. 84. This is the appropriate way to make your contact points on Print 1, but be sure you do not get any glue on the windows, since the windows on this print will show through on the final picture.

Cut round random leaves to define the shape of the tree branches on the top left of the picture. Clear out some of the spaces between the leaves and then remove from the print.

Place your mounds of glue on Print 1 as in Illus. 84. Be sure you avoid getting any glue in the window areas. Line up the house, first checking to see that the windows match exactly so that the rest of the cutting will be positioned properly. Next, pat down the bottom

Illus. 85.

of the house so that it rests directly on the base picture. Angle the top so that it comes out farther than the bottom. Check the tree and grass for alignment. Put the glue on the tree branches that go on the left of the picture so that you do not get any in the spaces you have cut between the leaves.

Print 3

In this print start again with the windows. Illus. 85 shows how to cut the units from the print. This time, cut out the curtains and spaces but leave the shades and the various objects in the different windows. Leave the door and dormer window uncut. Remove the grass behind the porch of the house, but leave the bush next to it uncut. Then cut out the house. Glue the house as you did before by aligning the windows with the print underneath.

Cut the large tree the same way as on Print 2, and remove some of the spaces between the leaves. Here, you can disregard the swing ropes—you do not need them from this print. However, cut out the girl on the swing and set her aside.

Treat the tree branches on the left as though they are bare branches. Follow the outline of each branch, disregarding the leaves—just cut right through them. Illus. 86 shows the depth you can achieve by doing the branches this way. The whole tree is on the bottom layer, the defined shape of the leaves on the second layer, and the outline of the branches is on the third level. When the glue has dried, gently mingle both layers together with your fingers. This produces an excellent effect.

Cut out in one piece the small section of grass in the lower right-

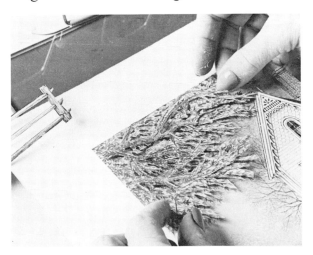

Illus. 86. Here is an effective way to treat trees in any picture you might want to work on. On the third print, simply follow the lines of the branches, just as though there were no leaves at all. The leaves will show through from the second print, and the whole—the branches and leaves—will show through from the basic print.

Illus. 87. Be sure to cut out the spaces between the flowers and stems from your third print.

Illus. 88. Since you will want a higher elevation for the top of the fence than the bottom, use larger mounds of glue at the top.

hand part of the picture. Before removing from the print, cut out the spaces between the flowers and then cut round the flowers and stalks (Illus. 87).

As shown in Illus. 88, cut out the fence and shrubbery in one piece. Glue the bottom of the fence closer to the picture than the top. To do this, simply put a larger mound of glue on the top than on the bottom.

Print 4

Remove everything from the windows except the frames. This includes the dormer window and the door window, too. Carefully cut the top, left side and bottom of the door so that you can open it just enough to lift it away from the picture. Using the tip of the blade, cut between the grillwork on top of the roof. This is delicate work, so take your time. Try to clear away enough space between the lines so that the result is an ornamental design rather than just one straight mass.

Check the original picture and you will see that the façade of the house is on different levels. To duplicate that effect, start by removing the left side of the house, and then cut out the rest of the house in one piece. Before layering, you can put "glass" in the windows by glueing clear plastic on the back as shown in Illus. 89. Do this in one piece for each section. Just cut the plastic slightly smaller than the structure of the section you are glueing it to.

Illus. 89. In any picture that has glass of any kind, you can simulate it easily by using pieces of clear plastic on the back of the cutting. Here, "glass" windows are being glued in place.

Glue the two sections of the house, elevating the left side more than the right so that there is a decided difference in level.

Cut out the wooden fence without the shrubs. Before you layer, bend it so that it follows the angle of the original picture.

Cut out the daisies individually, and put in place with tweezers as shown in Illus. 90.

Now for the final cutting of the large tree. This is painstaking, but the final effect is well worth the effort and time. Follow the outline of the branches (similar to the bare-branch method you used before) and cut as many of the large and small branches and twigs as you have the patience to do (Illus. 91). Place glue on the thickest part, that is the trunk. After the glue dries, lift the branches away from the tree. This adds greatly to the depth of the picture.

Illus. 90 (left). For delicate pieces such as these individual daisy cuttings, use your tweezers. Illus. 91 (right). If you have the time and the inclination, cut out all the branches and twigs, using the bare-branch technique.

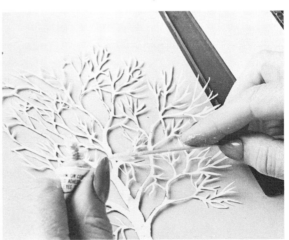

Print 5

Start on the fifth print by cutting out the intricate design on the white decorative peak of the house and remove from the print. Using the tip of the blade, cut just enough to define the design. Glue to the house as in Illus. 92. Remove the awning from the large window on the same side of the house as the peak and glue in place. Remove the roof by cutting up to the grillwork. You can cut right through the dormer since you still have the one you put aside from Print 2. Glue the roof at an angle, the top part level with the grillwork, and the bottom elevated so that it comes out farther than the windows beneath it. Next cut out the little roof on the dormer. Glue the entire dormer from Print 2 to the roof, and then glue the dormer roof in the same way as the main roof.

Now remove the porch roof with the posts attached. Crease the roof slightly above the decorative design. Place just a tiny dab of glue on the bottoms of the posts and use large mounds on the roof. When the porch is in place, press the bottom of the posts down so that they rest on the porch floor (Illus. 93). This helps position the upper part of the porch roof so that it distinctly juts out over the porch in a natural way.

The placement of the left side of the house and the two roofs give the house the needed variance in depth levels that the picture requires.

Illus. 92. On your fifth print, you must remove the most delicate part first—in this case, the intricate woodwork on the peak of the house.

Illus. 93. When you remove the porch roof with the posts attached, be sure to crease the roof slightly. Set the cutting in place and position the posts so they are on the floor of the porch.

Illus. 94. And here is the finished "White House," looking inviting enough to walk right into.

Now you can cut out and glue the three bushes and the steps in front of the house. Contour the bushes first. Then cut out the swing section, complete with ropes, and glue. Add the second figure of the girl from Print 3 as soon as the glue dries.

Cut out and add the smaller shrubs on the fence. Cut out the flowers on the large bush individually and put in their proper place on the bush.

For an extra touch, place glue on small, dried straw flowers and scatter them in front of the fence and against the house.

Spray with sealer and your picture is ready for framing.

9. "Sleigh Ride"

THE DRAMATIC WINTER SCENE in Illus. 97 is dominated by the large tree in the foreground. The intertwining branches call for close attention to detail, but they are not difficult to do. Use four prints, glueing the first to the back-board. To help preserve the appearance of snow, do not darken any cut edges in the picture except those of the large tree trunk.

Print 2

Cut away all patches of blue sky. This means cutting within the branches of all the trees. You can disregard some of the fine twigs when you are cutting since they appear on the basic print and will show through the various layers. Do not cut branches that come in contact with other units of the picture, such as the buildings, snow, and the dense foliage at the far back of the picture.

After this, cut out the frozen stream in the foreground, leaving the banks of snow on both sides as shown in Illus. 95. This illustration also shows a slit you must make now between the rocks on the far bank and the bridge.

Cut the mounds of snow that are piled against the tree in the foreground. Cut to the base of the tree and round the bottom so that the snow is part of the bank. Contour the snow as in Illus. 96. (The next layers of the trees will be glued behind these snow mounds.)

Illus. 95 (left). Cutting out the stream from Print 2. Illus. 96 (below). Notice the contoured snow at the base of the tree at the left of the photo.

Copyright Donald Art Company, Inc.

Illus. 97. The original print, as you can see, lacks depth.

Illus. 98. Now, look at the difference!

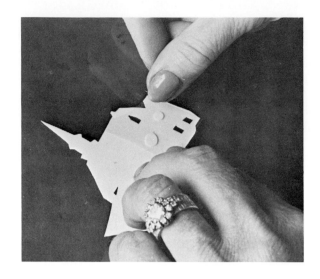

Illus. 99 (left). The church receives some "glass" (plastic) windows. Illus. 100 (above). Glue the branches in place carefully.

Release the picture from the print and contour both banks of snow so that they are high in the middle and incline towards the edges. Layer your picture as in Illus. 96. The banks of snow will touch on the stream and still have enough variance in height to make a noticeable difference between the level of the water and the land. Do not glue the snow mounds to the tree in this layering.

Print 3

To the left of the big tree are two houses, a tree and part of the bridge. Cut these units out in one piece. Leave the trunk of the tree attached to the houses. Cut out the branches at random. There are so many, and they are so close together it is not possible to separate them all. Even if you did, the ends of the branches would be so thin and fragile they would tear. When you have glued this section to the picture, pull some of the branches forward and away from the background.

Cut out the church and bridge as one unit. Empty the space within the windows and glue a small piece of clear plastic to the back of the church for window glass as shown in Illus. 99. When layering, tuck the end of the bridge behind the slit that you made on Print 2 and be sure that you press the house next to the church behind the tree.

Work with the barn unit on the right side of the picture next. Remove the two buildings and the tree in one section, but do not cut out the part of the trunk or any of the branches that rest against the buildings. However, cut as many of the branches as you can, going right through the branches of the big middle tree as though they were not there. Again you can ignore the very smallest of the twigs. Glue and place as in Illus. 100.

Remove the large patches of snow from the branches of the middle tree and put aside. Do the same with the branches that are growing on top and appear closest to your eye as you look at the tree. Now cut out what remains of the tree and glue it behind the mound of snow.

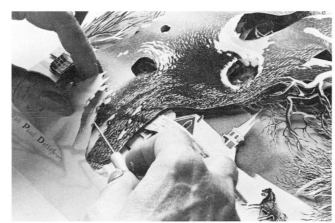

Illus. 101. From Print 4, cut out and glue the middle tree behind the layered mound of snow resting against it.

Print 4

Cut out the church steeple, the front section of the bridge on both sides of the tree, the horse and sleigh, and the small building in the forefront of the barn unit. Glue all of these into place. Start on the middle tree, cutting all branches to completion including the ones that bisect the other trees. Remove the tree in front of the barn with just its trunk and a few of the main offshoots that remain when the other tree is completed. Remove the narrow mound of snow that borders the bank at the water's edge and the small bush at the extreme right of the picture.

Again glue the middle tree behind the mound of snow (Illus. 101). When the tree is in place, curve the snow with your fingers so that it rests against the tree. As in Illus. 101, add the patches of snow and the branches you had put aside from Print 3. Now put the remaining part of the second tree in place in front of the barn, contour the narrow mound of snow and glue in place in front of the tree. Add the bush. With a thin stick or similar tool, gently mingle the branches from both trees and raise a few so that they come forward and out.

Illus. 102. Here is a birthday card on which the message does not interfere with the picture.

10. Greeting Cards

You CAN FIND an almost endless variety of subjects for three-dimensional decoupage pictures in greeting-card shops. Just before a

Illus. 103. Pink construction paper was used as a backing for the basic cutting from Illus. 102. Four identical cards produced this three-dimensional effect.

special holiday such as Easter, Valentine's Day or Christmas, especially beautiful cards are on display, and usually cost less than prints.

Christmas offers an abundance of riches since you can buy cards by the box. If they are sold in dozen lots you can make three pictures per box—an inexpensive and original way to make gifts for family or friends.

Why not start a three-dimensional collection of the Christmas cards you send out each year? You will have attractive decorations that, in time, will be a nostalgic record of past holidays. Be sure to put the date on the front of the finished project after it is sprayed with sealer.

Before you choose a card, be sure that you check on the texture of the paper. Some cards are made of paper that is close to cardboard in thickness, and you will not be able to cut through them with ease or do any shaping; others are too light a quality that would tear and also resist shaping. Try to choose cards that are as close as possible to the texture of the prints with which you have been working.

Original card courtesy of Regency Thermographers of California, Inc.

Illus. 104. This partridge in a pear tree has a foil backing. Foil is very pliable, so be sure to avoid an exaggerated effect when contouring. Smooth down each unit lightly before glueing.

Illus. 105. For this wise old owl, use the methods you learned when working with birds and trees (Illus. 42).

Illus. 106. This whimsical three-dimensional picture would add a charming touch to a child's room.

The best cards to buy are those without any greeting across the front. Occasionally you will find one that you just must have that does have a message on the face of the card. If the words do not interfere with any important sections of the picture, you can cut it out and transfer it to another backing (Illus. 102).

Four cards are usually sufficient for decoupaging, but if you find one with great detail such as in Illus. 105, buy five. If you do not use it for your picture, chances are you will find an occasion to send it to someone, so be sure you take the envelopes when you buy your cards.

Illus. 106 is one of an original series of four greeting cards that lend themselves beautifully to decoupaging. The message is inside the card and there is no problem in having to transfer the pictures. Illus. 106 is part of a series which can make a whimsical group that would fit nicely into a child's room. Individually, they make unusual baby shower gifts, ones that you could be certain would not duplicate other gifts.

Original Pictures

YOU MAY WISH to mark a special occasion or give a gift to someone with a picture that has personal significance and find that there is nothing available to suit your needs. You can compose your own pictures by using or combining parts of greeting cards, illustrations from books or magazines, calendar pictures, or just about anything that presents a workable surface, not too thin so that it tears easily nor so thick that you cannot cut properly.

Also, save the bits and pieces from used prints—you never know when you will need an extra flower, article of clothing, and so on. If you have sewing remnants, or worn clothing that you plan to discard check if the material is suitable as a backing for pictures and put some away for future use.

11. "The Poor Poet"

PRINTS OF FINE PAINTINGS and famous works of art are readily available for three-dimensional decoupage. Although some of these prints cost a bit more than other prints, the quality of the paper makes them a joy to work with and, of course, the colors are truer to the original painting than in the less expensive copies.

There is no difference in the methods you use in doing copies of museum reproductions. Study the picture well and sometimes you will discover that some of the most famous paintings in the world are the easiest to do in three-dimensions. The clarity of the original painting shows up in the copies of the print, and by following the artist-indicated levels of elevation, you will have little chance of going astray.

Illus. 107 shows a print that is a copy of Carl Spitzweg's, "The Poor Poet." Illus. 108 shows the picture done in three dimensions. Each detail was carefully observed and copied, from the tears in the pillow to separating and re-assembling the boards in the rafters.

Whichever fine painting suits your fancy you are certain to derive much pleasure from making it three-dimensional. Always make certain that your matting and framing are in keeping with the subject matter and the proportions of the picture you choose.

Illus. 107. "The Poor Poet," by Carl Spitzweg. Like many fine paintings, this one offers a wonderful opportunity for you to exercise your inventiveness.

Illus. 108. Notice how even the tiniest details have been put into the third dimension.

12. The Pictures of Anton Pieck

A BOOK ON THREE-DIMENSIONAL decoupage is not complete without some examples of the pictures of Anton Pieck. Pieck, who was born in 1895, is a Dutch artist whose pictures are especially suitable for decoupaging. Prints are available in all hobby and craft shops. He is prolific and the selection of prints is so large and varied that you are sure to find several that you would enjoy working with.

Some of his scenes depict the romance and charm we associate with previous centuries. He gives meticulous attention to details, and his pictures stand as an accurate record of an historical period.

This artist has an impressive background in the techniques of oil painting, engraving, lithography, etching and making woodcuts. You will find that many of these skills will be duplicated in the appearance of your completed project. The buildings, people, and

Original print copyright Donald Art Company, Inc.

Illus. 109. "The Tavern." The background consists of the buildings on the side of the tavern and needs only one layering. The diamond-shaped window-panes call for careful cutting, so take your time.

Illus. 110. ''The Toy Store.'' Cut out the carriage wheels using the same method for cutting out window-panes.

Illus. 111. ''The Apothecary Shop.'' Remember to glue the objects on the tables at a slight angle so that the bottoms rest close to the table and the tops are elevated.

objects in his pictures call for your close attention. The longer you study your picture, the more you will see. The areas for elevation are clearly delineated and you will have no difficulty in deciding on the height of the layering you will want to do.

The three examples shown here were made with five copies of each print. The extra print allows you to give full scope to all the features that the artist portrays. Usually it is unnecessary to add any additional touches as these pictures are so complete in themselves.

Index